Cake Pop Recipes

Even Beginners Can Make

Prepare Tasty Cake Pop Treats with These Simple Recipes

BY: Nancy Silverman

COPYRIGHT NOTICES

Table of Contents

Introduction

You really don't need to be a pro if you want to amaze everyone with a special dessert. Cake pops are everyone's favorite, so you can play it safely. In this cookbook, you will find out many secrets that will help you during the preparation process. We will reveal the best flavor combinations, and no one will believe that they are eating an effortless and quick dessert. Whether it is a wedding reception, a birthday, or graduation, be sure that this decorative dessert will be spoken of for a long time. Everyone will like to know the recipe for a brownie cake pop. They will also ask for the red velvet cake pops too. Don't forget to display them nicely on your party, as they are very pretty. Let's get started now!

1. Strawberry cheesecake cake pops

Do you love the taste of the classic cheesecake? Now, you can try it in a different shape. Make sure that all the ingredients listed below are at room temperature, as it will be easier to incorporate them this way.

Servings: 14

Cooking time: 8 hours

Ingredients:

- 16 oz. cream cheese, room temperature
- 1/2 cup powdered sugar
- 5 Tablespoons granulated sugar
- 1 teaspoon vanilla extract
- 1/2 cup sour cream
- 3/4 cup strawberries, chopped on small pieces
- Grounded graham crackers

Instructions:

Mix the 16 oz cream cheese with an electric mixer. Add 4 tablespoons of powdered sugar and mix until well combined.

Add vanilla and sour cream. Mix well again.

Sprinkle the strawberries with one tablespoon of powdered sugar. Add into the mixture and mix lightly. Leave it in the fridge overnight or 8 hours.

Remove and let it soften for 20 minutes. Take a small handful of the cheesecake mixture and shape it into a ball. Place them on a pan and put in the freezer for a short time. Roll them in your hands again to form the balls.

Cover the balls with grounded graham crackers. Stick a kabob stick.

2. Confetti cake pops

Whether you need a good recipe for party foods or just a treat for your kids, this is it. The colorful cake pops will make everyone fall in love with them. The recipe is quite easy so that anyone can do it. Let's get going!

Servings: 24

Cooking time: 4 hours

Ingredients:

- 1 box Strawberry Cake Mix
- 1/2 container Vanilla Frosting
- 1 bag White Chocolate Candy Melts
- 1 handful of Rainbow Sprinkles

Instructions:

Follow the instructions on the strawberry cake mix package and cook the cake mix. When it is done, let it cool down.

When the cake is cooled down, crumble it. Fold in the frosting slowly until you reach a nice dough that can be easily shaped with your hands.

Shape the balls. Melt the white chocolate.

Dip a cake pop stick into the chocolate. Then insert it into the ball. Repeat with all of them and let it harden.

Dip the cake pops in the white chocolate. Sprinkle with the sprinkles and let the chocolate harden in the fridge.

3. Chocolate covered cake pops truffles

The great thing about this cake pop recipe is that you can use any leftover cake. You can choose your favorite recipe or buy a pack at the store. You have complete freedom, according to the time that you have.

Servings: 36

Cooking time: 1 hour 30 minutes

Ingredients:

- 15.25 oz yellow cake mix
- 18 tablespoons buttercream frosting
- 12 ounces of chocolate melting disks
- 1 cup rainbow sprinkles

Instructions:

Bake the cake according to the instructions. Let it cool completely and crumble it. Mix with the frosting and ½ cup sprinkles.

Roll into tablespoon-sized balls. Let the cake pop truffles harden in the freezer for an hour.

Melt the chocolate. Dip the top of each ball in chocolate using a fork. Tap to shake off the excess and place on parchment paper. Add sprinkles on top and let them harden completely.

4. Brownie cake pops

If you prepare a store-bought mix as brownies, everyone will notice it. But, if you adjust the recipe slightly, you will have these tasty pop cake balls. No one will ever guess that you have made it by using the store-bought cake mix!

Servings: 16

Cooking time: 3 hours 30 minutes

Ingredients:

- Sprinkles
- 2 teaspoons shortening
- Lollipop sticks
- 1 bag (9.5 oz) Dove Silky Smooth Dark Chocolate
- 1 box family-size fudgy brownie mix

Instructions:

Bake the chocolate fudge brownie mix according to the package instructions. Let it cool for an hour after removing from the oven. Trim off the edges so that you have a soft cake to work with.

In a mixing bowl, crumble the brownies. Use a cookie scoop to shape the mixture into balls. Smoothen them with your hands and place them on a baking paper-lined pan.

Insert a stick onto each one and freeze for 2 hours.

Melt the chocolate together with the shortening. Stir while doing so.

Dip the cake pops in chocolate and let them harden in the fridge.

5. Ice cream cone cake pops

Do you want to prepare a pretty looking dessert that kids will love? These cake pops are looking so decorative but are so easy to make. You can serve them on a birthday party or offer them as a bribe treat to kids.

Servings: 15

Cooking time: 20 minutes

Ingredients:

- Sprinkles
- 16 oz. dark chocolate canned frosting
- 12 oz candy melts
- 9.5 oz. Dark Chocolate
- 15 red candies
- 15 small ice cream cones
- 15.25 oz dark chocolate cake mix

Instructions:

First, Prepare the cake according to the instructions. Let it cool down completely before proceeding.

Crumble the cake and put it into the large bowl. Add half of the can of frosting and mix well. Add more if you need it.

Use a cookie scoop to shape the cake pop balls. Place them on a paper-lined pan. Then cool for an hour in the fridge.

Use the remaining cake mix to fill the ice cream cones. Set them aside.

Melt the candy melts. Dip the top edges of the cone in chocolate.

Dip the bottom of a cake ball into the chocolate. Then, place it in the cone. Repeat with all and set them aside to cool down.

Melt the hardened leftover candy melts again. Dip the balls to cover them completely. Set aside and cool down.

Melt the dark chocolate. Spoon a little of the chocolate over the top of the balls. Add a red candy on top and allow it to cool completely.

6. Blue velvet cake pops

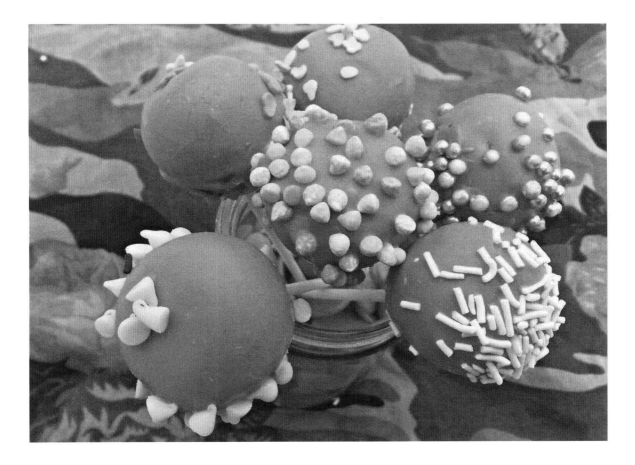

This dessert is perfect for a boy's birthday party or even a baby shower. The blue color looks so amazing, so you can even serve them at a sea-themed party. The possibilities are endless, so make sure that you don't miss this stunning recipe!

Servings:30

Cooking time: 3 hours

Ingredients:

- 16.5 oz box of blue velvet cake mix
- 12 oz vanilla frosting
- 21 oz blue melting wafers
- White sprinkles

Instructions:

Bake cake according to instructions. Let it cool completely before you crumble it.

In a mixing bowl, mix the crumbles with the frosting. Shape into balls and cool them in the fridge.

Melt the blue wafers. If the mixture is too thick, you can use shortening.

Dip a stick into melted wafers and insert it into a cake pop. Repeat with all of them and let to harden.

Dip the whole pop cakes in the melted wafers. Sprinkle with sprinkles and let them harden.

7. Cool galaxy cake pops

Do you want to make the unique and decorative cake pops? This recipe will show you how to do it. The galaxy cake balls are so easy to make. All you need to do is be a little creative and follow this simple recipe!

Servings: 12

Cooking time: 40 minutes

Ingredients:

- 5 cups white cake crumbled
- 1/3 cup white frosting
- 12 oz. white chocolate melting wafers
- 4 oz. blue chocolate melts
- 4 oz. purple chocolate melts
- 4 oz. black chocolate melts
- Silver Sugar Crystals Sprinkles
- Tiny Gold Star Sprinkles

Instructions:

In a large mixing bowl, mix the cake crumbles a frosting. Shape mixture into one-inch balls. Stack them on a baking paper-lined pan.

Melt the white chocolate. Dip a stick in the chocolate and insert into cake balls. Repeat with all of them and let it harden.

Melt the different colored candy melts in different bowls. Drizzle black and blue over the white chocolate. Dip the cake balls in the mixture to cover them. Sprinkle with starts and the sugar. Let them harden.

8. Easy Oreo cake pops

Do you love the rich chocolate taste and crunchiness of Oreo? You can now prepare your favorite recipe with these treats. Everyone will like to have a bite of the chocolate goodness, so make sure that you prepare enough for them.

Servings: 15

Cooking time: 45 minutes

Ingredients:

- dark chocolate, melted
- 4 oz cream cheese softened
- 24 Oreo cookies
- 2 tbsp candy melting aid to thin out the candy
- 12 oz white candy melts

Instructions:

Add the Oreos in a blender. Pulse until they are finely crumbled. Add the cream cheese and pulse again to mix. Pour the mixture in a bowl.

Scoop out the small cake balls. Shape them with your hands to get smooth and beautiful balls.

Align them onto a sheet lined with paper. Freeze for about fifteen minutes.

Melt the white candy melts. Coat the tip of a stick and insert it into a cake ball. Repeat with each and let them cool again for 5 mins.

Melt the candy melts again, s the mixture can harden. Add in melting aid and mix well to get a thinner consistency.

Coat the cake balls with melted mixture. Tap to remove excess. Drizzle with some melted chocolate chips on top. Let them harden.

9. Champagne cake pops

Are you looking for a stylish and elegant dessert? This recipe will amaze you for sure. The pink champagne cake balls will definitely surprise all of your guests. They can be served at a party or even a wedding reception.

Servings:60

Cooking time: 3 hours

Ingredients:

- 1 Pink Champagne Cake
- 1 batch Pink Champagne Buttercream
- 32 ounces white chocolate
- ½ - 1 cup diamond sugar

Instructions:

Crumble the cake into fine crumbs. Add the pink champagne buttercream. Mix well until incorporated.

Scoop out the pink champagne cake balls and place them on a baking paper-lined sheet. With your hands, shape them into sweet round balls.

Freeze for two hours.

Melt the white chocolate in the micro or a water bath.

Dip the tip of each stick and stick it into the balls. Let it harden. Dip the cake balls in the chocolate and tap gently to remove excess.

Sprinkle with sugar and let them cool and harden.

10. Cookie dough cake pops

There are so many variations of the cake pop recipes. Don't forget to try the cookie dough version. It is sweet, versatile, and incredibly delicious. The creamy and fudgy inside will make you crave for more and more.

Servings:22

Cooking time: 1 hour

Ingredients:

- 1 3/4 cup all-purpose flour
- 1 cup unsalted butter, softened
- 1 1/2 cup brown sugar
- 1/4 cup sugar
- 1 teaspoon vanilla extract
- 1/2 teaspoon salt
- 1/2 cup mini chocolate chips
- 10 oz dark chocolate melting wafers

Instructions:

Beat the softened butter, brown sugar, and white sugar until smooth and creamy.

Add the salt and vanilla extract and mix well.

Do the sifted flour gradually. Add the chocolate chips and stir.

Scoop the mixture into tiny cake balls and roll them with your hands. Stack on a paper-lined sheet and place it in the fridge for 20 minutes.

Prepare the melting wafers according to instructions. Dip the stick in and insert it into the ball. Once it is hardened, dip the cake ball in the chocolate. Leave them in the fridge to set.

11. Margarita cake pops

Do you need a fun summer dessert that everyone will love? These margarita cake pops are the perfect dessert. Whether it is a summer party or just a gathering by the pool, you now have an opportunity to try this recipe.

Servings:24

Cooking time: 1 hour 20 minutes

Ingredients:

- Juice and zest of 2 limes, divided
- Coarse sparkling sugar, for decoration
- 1 box vanilla cake mix
- 1/4 triple sec, plus 1 teaspoon
- 1 pack key lime frosting
- 12 oz bag white candy melts
- 1/2 cup tequila plus, 1 Tablespoon
- 1/4 cup powdered sugar

Instructions:

Prepare the store-bought vanilla cake mix according to the instructions. In the mixture, add ½ cup tequila, ¼ cup triple sec, zest and juice from one lime. Bake according to instructions.

When cooled, crumble the cake. Add in the rest of the tequila, triple sec, and buttercream. Add the sugar and mix well. Leave it for half an hour to chill.

Shape the dough into small balls and place them over a paper-lined sheet.

Melt the candy melts. Cover the balls in the chocolate. Allow it to drip to remove the excess. Sprinkle with lime zest and coarse sugar.

12. Watermelon cake pops

Do you need a stunning summer dessert that everyone will love? These watermelon cake pops will amaze your summer party guests. The sweet pink inside part comes with a green outer layer. If you plan to throw a watermelon themed or summer themed party, you have the recipe for the treats.

Servings:24

Cooking time: 1 hour 20 minutes

Ingredients:

- 1 box strawberry cake mix
- 1 cup water
- 1/3 cup vegetable oil
- 1 cup buttercream frosting
- 1/2 c. mini semi-sweet chocolate chips
- 1 - 12 oz. bag green candy melts

Instructions:

Prepare the store-bought strawberry cake mix according to the instructions. Bake according to instructions.

When cooled, crumble the cake. Add in the buttercream, one spoon at a time. Add gradually until you reach the desired consistency. Mix in the chocolate chips.

Shape the dough into small balls and place them over a paper-lined sheet. Leave them for half an hour to chill.

Melt the candy melts. Cover the balls in the chocolate. Allow it to drip to remove the excess. Allow the chocolate to set for 20 minutes.

13. Cookies and cream cake pops

Are you craving for your favorite dessert cookies and cream? Now you can experience the sweet, yummy, and creamy taste of this dessert in a whole new way. These cake pops will amaze even the most sophisticated taste buds.

Servings: 15

Cooking time: 60 minutes

Ingredients:

- 4 cups vanilla cake, crumbled
- 1 cup Oreo cookies, finely crushed
- 1/2 cup vanilla buttercream
- 1 12 oz bag white chocolate chips
- 24 oz semi-sweet chocolate chips

Instructions:

Prepare the cake according to instructions. Once cooled, crumble it. Divide 4 cups of the crumbs in a bowl.

Add ½ cup buttercream and ¾ of the Oreos. Mix well until incorporated and chill for about an hour in the fridge.

Scoop out some of the cake ball mixtures and roll it in balls with your hands.

Melt the semi-sweet chocolate chips. Dip a stick in the chocolate, and then stick it into a ball. Repeat with al and let it harden.

Dip the balls in the chocolate. Allow the chocolate to set up. Melt the white chocolate in the micro, and dip the cake balls halfway in.

Sprinkle with crushed Oreo and leave to chill.

14. Oatmeal cream cake pops

This is a unique recipe that most of you will fall for. The crunchy and creamy dessert will amaze the pickiest dessert lovers. All you have to do to enjoy the yumminess is to head to the kitchen now!

Servings: 18

Cooking time: 30 minutes

Ingredients:

- 1 box little oatmeal cream pies
- 8 oz white chocolate

Instructions:

Add the oatmeal pies in a food processor. Pulse until you reach to fine crumbs.

Remove ¼ for decorations. Add the rest into a bowl. Scoop out some of the mixtures and shape them in small balls with your hands.

Align the balls on a paper-lined sheet. Pop in the fridge for 10 minutes.

Melt the chocolate in the microwave or using a double boiler.

Create a hole into each ball with a stick. Dip a lollipop stick into the chocolate, and then stick into the ball. Leave them to chill for 5 mins.

Coat the balls with chocolate. Sprinkle with the rest of the crumbs and let them chill.

15. Strawberry cake pops

Strawberries are an excellent addition to desserts. Here we have a delicious, fruity, and mouthwatering strawberry cake ball recipe that you will absolutely love. Prepare it in less than an hour and enjoy it with family and friends.

Servings:24

Cooking time: 55 minutes

Ingredients:

- 1 box strawberry cake mix
- 2 tablespoons vanilla frosting
- 1/2 cup freeze-dried strawberries
- 1 cup powdered sugar

Instructions:

Prepare the cake according to the instructions indicated on the package. Let it cool down completely and crumble it into a large mixing bowl.

Add the strawberries into the bowl. Add the frosting and mix. Add more frosting if the mixture is crumbly.

Take two tablespoons of the mixture and roll them into a ball.

Add the powdered sugar in a small bowl. Cover the balls in powdered sugar.

16. S'more cake pops

Do you love the rich taste of the classic S' mores? Now you can have your favorite dessert in a whole new way. These cake balls will amaze every picky dessert lover!

Servings: 24

Cooking time: 1 hour

Ingredients:

Ganache center:

- 16 oz good quality milk chocolate
- 8 oz heavy whipping cream
- Graham crackers crushed

White marshmallow over:

- 3 egg whites
- 1/2 teaspoon cream of tartar
- 2 tablespoons sugar
- 1/3 Cup water
- 3/4 Cup light corn syrup
- 2/3 Cup sugar
- 1 teaspoon vanilla extract

Instructions:

First, prepare the ganache for the cake balls. Chop the chocolate bar into tiny pieces and place in a mixing bowl.

Heat the cream and bring to simmer. Pour the heated whipping cream over the chocolate and let it melt for 5 mins. Mix well.

Place in the fridge to cool down and firm.

Scoop some of the ganache and roll into balls. Insert a stick and cover with graham crackers.

Prepare the marshmallow layer. Beat the cream of tartar together with the egg whites. Gradually pour in the 2 Tablespoons of sugar and continue to beat until soft peaks form.

In a pan, heat the corn syrup, water, and sugar and bring to a boil. Heat to 242 degrees, and then remove.

Gradually pour the hot syrup into the beaten egg whites while beating on low. Increase to high and beat for 4 minutes.

Add vanilla and beat for three more mins, or until it is thick.

Dip the balls into the marshmallow. Toast each one with a brulee torch.

17. Gluten-free cake pops

Are you looking for a tasty and decadent gluten-free version of the popular dessert? This is the right pick. Maybe you have someone that doesn't consume gluten, or you want to offer this option at the party for any case. Don't forget to label this dessert as a gluten-free option, so that everyone knows.

Servings: 12

Cooking time: 2 hours

Ingredients:

- 2 cups gluten-free chocolate cake
- 1/2 cup vanilla frosting
- 1 1/2 cups good quality dark chocolate, gluten-free

Instructions:

Add the gluten-free cake crumbs into a mixing bowl. Add frosting and mix the mixture with your hands.

Scoop some of the mixtures and make a ball. Stack the cake balls onto a paper-lined sheet.

Melt the chocolate using a double boiler or in the micro. Dip a lollipop stick into the chocolate, and then into the ball. Once hardened, dip each cake ball into the chocolate. Chill for one hour in the fridge.

18. Maraschino cherry cake pops

Do you want a tasty party dessert that has a nice presentation? With a maraschino cherry in the middle, this cake ball recipe is the one that will amaze everyone. The sweet note, together with the creamy frosting, will create a sweet harmony for your taste buds.

Servings: 12

Cooking time: 4 hours

Ingredients:

- 8oz Maraschino Cherries with a stem
- 1 Tub White Frosting
- 1 1/2 Cup Semi-Sweet Chocolate
- 1 Box White Cake Mix

Instructions:

Prepare the cake according to the instructions indicated on the package. Allow it to cool and trim off the brown edges.

Crumble the cake in a mixing bowl. Add half of the frosting and mix. Add some more if the mixture is too crumbly.

Shape balls in the size of a tablespoon. Align them on a paper-lined sheet.

Drain the maraschino cherries and dry them with a towel.

Carefully create a pocket with your fingers in each ball. Place a cherry inside and roll it in your hands to shape a nice round ball. The stem should peek outside.

Melt the chocolate and dip each ball inside, holding the cherry stem. Return them to the paper-lined sheet and place in the fridge to set for 3 hours.

19. Chocolate cheesecake cake pops

This decadent dessert has a creamy and sweet inside, and gooey chocolate on the outside. It is the perfect pick for the ones that are after a luxurious and rich taste. This is the right dessert that will amaze everyone!

Servings: 35

Cooking time: 5 hours 10 minutes

Ingredients:

- 5 large eggs
- 1/4 cup all-purpose flour
- 2 cups of sugar
- 1/4 cup sour cream
- 2 teaspoons vanilla extract
- 2 egg yolks
- Boiling water
- 2 pounds chocolate, chopped
- 4 tablespoons vegetable shortening
- 40 oz cream cheese, at room temperature
- 1/4 teaspoon salt

Instructions:

Preheat the oven to 325 degrees. Set water to boil.

Beat the cream cheese, flour, sugar, and salt until combined. Beat on low and add the eggs and egg yolks, one at a time. Beat in cream and vanilla too.

Pour in a pan and place over a larger pan. Add in the boiling water to cover half of the pan with the cake. Bake for about 45 to 55 minutes.

Cool to room temperature. Then, cool it for 3 hours in the fridge covered with plastic foil.

Scoop out the cake balls and place them over a paper-lined sheet. Add a stick and freeze them for about two hours.

Melt the chocolate. Dip the cake balls and tap them to remove the excess. If thickened, add shortening.

Let them refrigerate for 24 hours before serving.

20. Lime cake pops

This is a fresh and tasty version of the popular pop cake recipes. It is a simple summary version, so it can suit your summer parties. This sweet and sour will give the flavor a lift. Everyone will like to try these tasty key lime cake pops.

Servings: 40

Cooking time: 3 hours

Ingredients:

- 1 box key lime cake mix
- ½ cup key lime frosting
- 2 packages Vanilla CANDIQUIK Coating
- 3 drops of Lime oil
- Graham crackers, crumbled

Instructions:

Prepare the cake by following the instruction on the box.

Let it cool down completely and crumble it in a large mixing bowl, combine the cake crumbs with the frosting.

Shape with your hands to get one-inch balls. Place them over paper lined sheet and refrigerate for 1 to 2 hours.

Melt the CANDIQUIK according to the instructions indicated on the package. Add in the lime oil and mix well. Dip the cake balls and align them on the paper-lined sheet. Sprinkle with graham crackers and refrigerate until set.

21. Pumpkin spice cake pops

Do you need the perfect and simple recipe for an autumn dessert? This is the perfect pick for the ones that love the pumpkin flavor, accompanied by crunchy pecans.

Servings: 35

Cooking time: 2 hours

Ingredients:

- 2 8- or 9-inch baked pumpkin-flavored cake layers,
- 1/2 cup frosting
- 20 oz white candy melts.
- 1 cup pecans, chopped

Instructions:

Crumble the pumpkin-flavored cake in a large mixing bowl. Add ¼ cup frosting and mix well. If it is crumbly, add some more.

Take a heaping tablespoon from the mixture and shape a ball with your hands. Refrigerate the balls for two hours.

Melt a little of the candy melts. Dip the stick in, and then stick them into the balls. Chill for 15 minutes to harden.

Melt the candy melts. Cover the cake balls with chocolate. Dip into finely chopped pecans. Refrigerate until hardened.

22. Triple chocolate cake pops

Chocolate lovers will be amazed by this decadent recipe. Not one, but the types of chocolate are here to satisfy your sweet cravings. This dessert will tickle your taste buds and make them ask for more.

Servings: 36

Cooking time: 3 hours

Ingredients:

- 1 chocolate cake
- 1-2 cups chocolate frosting
- chocolate almond bark and chocolate chips

Instructions:

Crumble the cake into a large mixing bowl. Add 1/3 cup frosting and mix well. Continue to add little by little and mix. Work until you reach a nice dough that you can easily shape with your hands.

Use a scoop to shape the balls. Roll them in your hands to create perfect balls.

Line the cake balls on a paper-lined sheet. Freeze them for one hour.

Melt the same amount of almond bark and chocolate chips.

Stick a lollipop stick into each ball. Then cover them with chocolate. Place them in the fridge to harden for another hour.

23. Cake pops in a cone

The standard way to serve cake pops is to stick them onto a lollipop stick. But you can always be creative and find new ways to do it. And yes, you can serve them in small waffle cones. Check out how to do it!

Servings: 26

Cooking time: 3 hours

Ingredients:

- 15 oz chocolate cake
- 5 oz cream cheese
- Icing sugar
- 13 oz white chocolate
- Chocolate melts
- Blue coloring
- 30 mini waffle cones

Instructions:

Crumble the chocolate cake.

Beat the cream cheese until smooth. Add in ½ cup sifted icing sugar. Beat again to combine, and then add the cake crumbles. Roll into balls and let them chill in the freezer for 20 minutes.

Melt the white chocolate for dipping in a double boiler or in the microwave. Divide it into two bowls. Add 3 drops of blue food coloring to the one and mix. Dip the top of the cone is chocolate and stick the ball inside. Allow setting.

Dip the cake ball into the blue chocolate. Let it set in the fridge.

24. Lemon cake pops

If you love a good lemon pie, this recipe will become your favorite. The spongy lemon cake, together with the creamy frosting, will create a dessert that you will love. Perfect for that summer party or spring brunch.

Servings: 24

Cooking time: 1 hour 45 minutes

Ingredients:

- 1 9×13 lemon cake
- 1 tablespoon butter softened
- 2 oz cream cheese, softened
- 1 1/4 cups powdered sugar
- 1 teaspoon pure vanilla extract
- 1 tablespoon milk if needed
- 1 teaspoon lemon extract
- 1 Tablespoon lemon zest if desired
- 2 cups white chocolate chips

Instructions:

Combine butter, powdered sugar, cream cheese, and vanilla and lemon extract. If too stiff, add1/2 or 1 tablespoon milk. Add lemon zest also.

Crumble the cake and add it to the frosting.

Scoop out the balls and shape them with your hands. Leave them for 45 mins in the freezer.

Melt the white chocolate and dip the balls. Leave them in the freezer to set.

25. Carrot cake pops

You can never get enough of the popular dessert. It is all about getting creative, so now you should try with a carrot cake. The exotic taste will be loved by everyone!

Servings: 16

Cooking time: 1 hr. 15 mins

Ingredients:

- 1 1/2 cup carrot cake
- 1 cup cream cheese frosting
- 1 1/2 cup white chocolate chips
- orange sugar sprinkles

Instructions:

Crumble the cake into a mixing bowl.

Add in the frosting and combine well. Scoop out one-inch balls and freeze them for one hour. Then remove them and shape them with your hands to a perfect ball.

Get back in the freezer for a few minutes.

Melt half of the chocolate. Dip a lollipop stick in chocolate, and then in the ball. Let them set in the freezer and cover them completely with chocolate.

Let the balls harden for one hour.

26. Orange creamsicle cake pops

You can never have enough recipe options when it comes to cake pops. And now you should try with orange cake. The sweet citrus note will lift up the recipe, while the creamy cheese frosting will add decadence.

Servings: 40

Cooking time: 2 hours 30 mins

Ingredients:

- 16 oz Vanilla CANDIQUIK Coating
- 1 box orange cake mix
- Orange Sprinkles
- ½ cup buttercream frosting

Instructions:

Prepare the cake according to the instructions. Let it cool completely and crumble it.

Add it into a mixing bowl and combine it with frosting.

Roll into one-inch balls and freeze for one hour. Melt the Vanilla CANDIQUIK and dip them. Place on paper-lined sheet and sprinkle. Let them set.

27. Peppermint cake pops

Who is craving for the chocolatey center, covered with a crunchy crushed candy cane? This is one of the recipes that everyone will love. Both kids and adults will enjoy the favorite winter dessert.

Servings: 12

Cooking time: 2 hours

Ingredients:

- 2 cups crumbled chocolate cake
- 1 cup store-bought buttercream frosting
- 2 candy canes, crushed

Instructions:

Mix the cake crumbles with four tablespoons frosting. Scoop out some of the mixture and roll it with your hands. Arrange on a sheet lined with paper. Freeze for 20 minutes.

Cover with remaining frosting. Sprinkle with the crushed candy canes.

28. Pumpkin spice cake pops

Season desserts are quite popular. These pumpkin spice cake pops will amaze every pumpkin spice lover out there. They will remind you of those cozy autumn days when you want to cozy up in your blanket.

Servings: 12

Cooking time: 2 hours

Ingredients:

- 2 cups crumbled yellow cake
- 4 oz cream cheese, softened
- 1/2 cup canned pumpkin purée
- 1 tsp cinnamon
- 1/8 tsp allspice
- 1/4 tsp ground ginger
- 3 tbsp powdered sugar
- 1/2 tsp vanilla extract

Instructions:

beat together cream cheese, cinnamon, pumpkin purée, ginger, allspice, powdered sugar, and vanilla extract. Divide into two bowls and set the one aside.

Add in the cake crumbles in the first bowl. Mix well and shape into balls. Stack them on a paper-lined sheet and stick the lollipop sticks. Freeze for 30 minutes.

Cover with the rest of the frosting.

29. Vegan cake pops

If you want to offer a vegan version at your party, this is the recipe to hold onto. The rich flavor will amaze every vegan out there, and they will ask you for the full recipe for sure.

Servings: 15

Cooking time: 1 hour

Ingredients:

- 1 chocolate vegan cake mix
- 1 cup vegan butter or shortening
- 3 cup powdered sugar
- 2 teaspoon vanilla extract
- Dark chocolate vegan chips

Instructions:

Cream the vanilla and vegan butter until combined. Gradually add the powdered sugar.

Prepare the vegan cake according to the instructions and let it cool. Crumble it in a large mixing bowl.

Add little by little from the frosting. Work until you have a dough that you can easily shape.

Add the mixture in the fridge and let it sit for 15 minutes.

Shape the balls with your hands and stack them on a paper-lined sheet. Place them back in the fridge.

Melt the chocolate. Stick the lollipop stick onto each ball and cover them with chocolate. Chill again until set.

30. Healthy cake pops

Do you need a healthy version of the favorite cake pops? This easy recipe includes no baking, so you can try it right now. The simple ingredients will make it easier to work with, and your kitchen won't end up with a huge mess.

Servings: 15

Cooking time: 1 hour

Ingredients:

- 1/2 cup coconut flour
- 1 Tablespoon cocoa powder
- 2 Tablespoon vegan protein powder
- 1/2 cup almond milk
- 1/4 cup maple syrup
- 1/4 cup chocolate chips + 2 Tbsp coconut oil, melted together
- 1/2 cup chocolate chips
- 3 teaspoons coconut oil

Instructions:

In a mixing bowl, combine the coconut flour, almond milk, protein powder, cocoa powder, and maple syrup.

Add in the mixture of chocolate chips and coconut oil that is melted.

Scoop out one tablespoon of the mixture and roll it in balls.

Melt the last 1/2 cup chocolate chips and 3 teaspoons coconut oil to get a chocolate mixture. Dip the lollipop stick in it, and then stick it into the cake pop. chill for 20 minutes and cover the whole cake balls. Let it chill for 20 minutes.

Conclusion

It is a lot easier for you, now when you have these stunning recipes in your hands. Preparing popcakes is so easy and simple and be sure that even beginners can do it. These recipes include a ready cake mix for all the busy people out there. But if you have a really good cake recipe, feel free to make it by yourself. The same goes for the frosting too. You can grab a can of your favorite flavored frosting, but you can also prepare it by yourself. You have the complete freedom with these recipes, and we assure you that you can't go wrong.

Feel free to experiment and come up with your own version too. These recipes can be your guidelines, but you can also add a personal stamp to any recipe.

About the Author

Nancy Silverman is an accomplished chef from Essex, Vermont. Armed with her degree in Nutrition and Food Sciences from the University of Vermont, Nancy has excelled at creating e-books that contain healthy and delicious meals that anyone can make and everyone can enjoy. She improved her cooking skills at the New England Culinary Institute in Montpelier Vermont and she has been working at perfecting her culinary style since graduation. She claims that her life's work is always a work in progress and she only hopes to be an inspiration to aspiring chefs everywhere.

Her greatest joy is cooking in her modern kitchen with her family and creating inspiring and delicious meals. She often says that she has perfected her signature dishes based on her family's critique of each and every one.

Nancy has her own catering company and has also been fortunate enough to be head chef at some of Vermont's most exclusive restaurants. When a friend suggested she share some of her outstanding signature dishes, she decided to add cookbook author to her repertoire of personal achievements. Being a technological savvy woman, she felt the e-book realm would be a better fit and soon she had her first cookbook available online. As of today, Nancy has sold over 1,000 e-books and has shared her culinary experiences and brilliant recipes with people from all over the world! She plans on expanding into self-help books and dietary cookbooks, so stayed tuned!

Author's Afterthoughts

Thank you for making the decision to invest in one of my cookbooks! I cherish all my readers and hope you find joy in preparing these meals as I have.

There are so many books available and I am truly grateful that you decided to buy this one and follow it from beginning to end.

I love hearing from my readers on what they thought of this book and any value they received from reading it. As a personal favor, I would appreciate any feedback you can give in the form of a review on Amazon and please be honest! This kind of support will help others make an informed choice on and will help me tremendously in producing the best quality books possible.

My most heartfelt thanks,

Nancy Silverman

If you're interested in more of my books, be sure to follow my author page on Amazon (can be found on the link Bellow) or scan the QR-Code.

https://www.amazon.com/author/nancy-silverman

Printed in Great Britain
by Amazon